SONGS OF FREEDOM

An Anthology by Iranian and Afghan Women Poets

"This anthology features ten remarkable award-winning female poets who have fled regimes hostile to their lives and voices, and found refuge and freedom in democracies across the world – a diaspora of courageous women from Iran and Afghanistan unveiled through the power of the written word. Some poems speak of love, female desire, escape, childhood and the role of women, others of longings for lost family and home, personal trauma, estrangement, atrocity, war, torture, stoning and imprisonment, yet all stand as a testament to a struggle for creative survival; a right to self-expression. 'Our native soil draws all of us, by I know not what sweetness, and never allows us to forget,' wrote Ovid, exiled from his beloved Rome. These talented poets, also exiled from the sweetness of their native soil, find powerful voice in this moving and enlightened collection, deepening our appreciation of the freedoms we enjoy."

–**Chrys Salt**, MBE, poet, author of *Skookum Jim and The Klondike Gold Rush*

"*Songs of Freedom* is an important and powerful anthology that connects the personal and the political in the profound lyrical insights of the ten exiled women poets from Iran and Afghanistan into the immense struggles faced by women in their countries of origin. Crucially, exile enables the poets to erupt to speak out in their resistance to clerical rule in their former countries with its control of women's bodies and destinies, its frequent violence and its human rights abuses. Yet, the immersive poems also explore the nuances of the true self revealing past loves and a deep attachment for the countries in which the poets lived and from which they fled. The poems expressing trauma were surely challenging to create but the imagery used is unusual and imaginative. The prevalence of the representation of suffering and killing, with its motifs of blood, stoning, corpses and graves, is striking and inevitably many of the poems are permeated by sadness, weeping, mourning and longing. Importantly, through this innovative anthology the impassioned voices of the gifted women poets will be widely heard as they sing their songs of freedom."

–**Dr Jennifer Langer**, poet and Exiled Writers Ink founding director, author of *The Search*

"*Songs of Freedom* is a timely, resonant and impassioned literary engagement with the Woman, Life, Freedom movement. Contributions from a range of writers – novelists, poets, translators, critics – from the Iranian diaspora and beyond help us to understand how this revolutionary resistance movement is resonating around the world. Shahrzad Mojab's trenchant introductory essay – giving a political, historical and social context to the events – also points out that above all the uprising has been a powerful, emotional earthquake whose aftershocks still tremble around the world. Leading writers respond here through poetry – as witnesses, empathetic observers, story-tellers, using the power of their language to bring us close to the moment and explore its many dimensions. The contributions range from an epic, mythological story of maternal loss transformed into the erasure of a generation of 'unknown girls' to condensed narratives of violence and comradeship or exploration of love and death through the eyes of exile. This work reminds us that while autocratic regimes around the world seek to divide and isolate us, through imagination we can stand united in solidarity and hope."

–**Catherine Temma Davidson**, novelist and poet, author of *The Orchard*

"The wrenching death of Mahsa Amini and other women for confronting morality police with a lock of hair running free, or an unintentional baring of their heads, has provoked a gentle revolution, now commemorated in a powerful anthology on Woman, Life, Freedom, authored by ten poets of the Afghan-Iranian diaspora. All of the poets in this book exemplify different perspectives from their own experiences of censorship or abuse merely for being women."

–**Karen Melander Magoon**, poet and opera singer, author of *I Love Wine and other songs*

SONGS OF FREEDOM

An Anthology by Iranian and Afghan Women Poets

Curated by
Shirin Razavian & Rouhi Shafii

Introduction by Shahrzad Mojab

Afsana Press
London

First published in 2024
by Afsana Press Ltd, London
www.afsana-press.com

Typeset by Afsana Press Ltd

A CIP catalogue record for this book is available from the British Library

ISBN paperback: 978-1-0685377-0-7
ISBN e-book: 978-1-0685377-1-4

In memory of Jîna Mahsa Amini
An ode to the Woman, Life, Freedom movement in Iran, and to Afghan women who have suffered long under despotic rules.
To all women who oppose repression in any form.

"From the perspective of my 'safe European home', it is not the situation these poets have to constantly deal with that impresses me – anyone and everyone has a duty to be utterly empathetic with them for that. It's more that under such oppression, these poets, these women, manage to maintain the integrity of their line, their wit, their dissent and their aesthetic trajectory, soaked as these are in 'exilic consciousness'. The power and freedom they win back, inspire, dream of, possess or fight for, are inside these lines, in marrow of the poems themselves."
–**Matthew Caley**, poet, author of *To Abandon Wizardry*

Contents

"In Iran and Afghanistan, poetry has anciently been the voice of the people and the voice of resistance; this electrifying collection offers us crafted, lyrical, and daring voices that ache, soar, arouse, beckon, and inspire – voices that must be heard. The poetry of radical grief, radical resistance, radical Beauty amidst ruin, is a tradition that speaks to the POWER of poetry to both mourn and uplift, to question and connect, to stay rooted in both our truth and the heart-slaying metaphors of our place and our history – and gifts us an opportunity to share and honour the heart and soul of a people. The poets included in *Songs of Freedom* are brilliant, extraordinary. These poems bear profound witness, are a wakeup call, a cri de coeur, a whisper, a shout, an anguished howl, a summons. They reach back to the ancient underpinnings of all poetry, all over the world, and remind us that the origin – and destiny – of poetry has always, and ever, been incantatory and necessary."
–**Judyth Hill**, poet, Chair of PEN International Women Writers Committee, author of *Hardwired For Love*

INTRODUCTION

The Poetics of *Life* and *Freedom*

How to speak *to, at,* and *with* a colossal historical event; to be able to capture its essence and meaning; to identify its actors and inner working; and to understand its promises, desires, and hopes? I propose it entails to engage in a dialogue with and reflection on *time* and *place* of the event itself. It also requires a delicate balance of reverence and inquiry, a willingness to listen to the whispers of the past while boldly projecting the echoes of the future. To capture all of this, one must become a frame for the event's stories, a conduit for its truths, and a beacon for its promises.

The *time* is 16 September 2022. The *place* is the city of Tehran, Iran. Jîna Mahsa Amini, a 22-year-old Kurdish woman (born 21 September 1999), was arrested for 'improper' veiling by the 'morality police' and was brutally killed while in custody.

The *time* is 17 September 2022. The *place* is Aichi cemetery in the city of Saqqez, in Rojhilatê, the Kurdish region of Iran. Jîna is buried. Jîna means 'giving life' from the etymological root of Jin (woman). Her grave is inscribed with: *Dearest Jîna, you shall not die, your name will be a symbol/ a code.*

The time and place collapsed in one colossal event: Jîna Mahsa Amini, a *butterfly* [in Sorani Kurdish پەپوولە], is murdered by the state and a *revolutionary storm was sparked* by her fall.[1] A death giving

1 Shahrzad Mojab (2023). "A revolutionary storm sparked by the fall of a butterfly." *Studies in Political Economy*. 104:3, pp. 189-202.

life to a feminist movement known as *Jin, Jiyan, Azadi* (*Woman, Life, Freedom*). A powerful movement, named after an inspiring slogan that was first chanted by Kurdish women, embodies struggle for freedom and justice. *Jin, Jiyan, Azadi* has become a symbol of resistance, echoing the courage and determination of those who fight for freedom, equality, and justice. A life-giving death that transcended borders and limits while inspiring a collective cry for justice and sparking a feminist defiance worldwide. To truly capture the essence of such death giving life, we should speak to and about it with the humility of a seeker, asking it to reveal its deepest meanings, hidden desires, and promises. To do so, I begin with immersing myself in its social and historical contexts to feel its pulse and the collective heartbeat of those who lived through it. I also speak with empathy, acknowledging the pain and challenges of the struggle, while also celebrating the resilience and courage that define it.

The *Woman, Life, Freedom* movement does not merely express a single idea of ending compulsory veiling; it encapsulates demands for gender and national equality, for freedom of thought, expression, and activism, as well as secularism and a universal social welfare. Women were among the first and, in some ways, the most important groups of participants in the 1979 revolution in Iran. They were also the first social group to be suppressed violently by the newly formed Islamic Republic after the revolution. Suppressing and marginalising women was not a secondary matter for the Islamic regime; rather, it was one of the structural-political necessities to establish its rule and consolidate its power.

Conversely, suppressing women who were actively engaged in political struggles against the Pahlavi monarchy (1925-1979), was not an easy task for the newly established Islamic regime. Broadly speaking, from the early 20th century, the entire Middle East and North Africa (MENA) region had been influenced by various factors such as colonialism, modernism, capitalist-imperialism, nationalism, and socialism, leading to social transformations from within. Urban middle and upper-class women, who had long been confined to the 'private' sphere of home and family, began to demand participation in 'public' life. As a result, women transformed into a new social force that sought the fulfilment of their demands for rights and equality, necessitating a redistribution of power in both private and public spheres.[2] This immense force in Iran, which had been liberated by the revolutionary struggles, was determined not to 'go back'. To consolidate various forms of oppression against women, the Islamic Republic needed to confront the resistance of opposing forces such as students, writers, academics, national minorities, and the left groups. These measures were not only part of the nationwide suppression process but also a form of targeted retribution against the struggle and resistance of women, national minorities such as Kurds, Arabs, and Turkmans. The massacres of political prisoners in the 1980s which eliminated thousands of young men and women, mostly secular or religious left, was part of this retaliatory state violence.[3] Therefore, it is evident that women in Iran have been resisting compulsory veiling and other discriminatory Islamic laws for more than four decades. These laws infringe on their rights in various aspects of life, including divorce, custody, inheritance, property ownership, marriage, travel permits, political participation, access to public spaces like stadiums, jobs, and higher education. Still, Jîna's Uprising has a haunting quality; it stuns

2 Shahrzad Mojab (2022). "Women and revolution in the Middle East," in Suad Joseph and Zeina Zaatari (eds). Handbook on Women in the Middle East. New York: Routledge, pp. 197-211.

3 Nasser Mohajer (2020). *Voices of a Massacre: Untold Stories of Life and Death in Iran, 1988*. Oneworld Publications.

us. It directs us toward the dynamic and complex nature of women's struggle in Iran for a century, in particular since the 1979 Revolution.

In the hundred-year history of women's struggles in Iran, as well as in the entire Middle East and North Africa, we have not witnessed such a widespread revolt against compulsory veiling. This uprising has undeniably transformed Iran's political landscape and stands as a historic turning point. We now refer to Iran as "pre-Jîna-Mahsa Amini" and "post-Jîna-Mahsa Amini" to reflect the historical, political, and social significance of this event. Though, initially sparked by a revolt against the compulsory hijab and patriarchal theocratic rule, the uprising has also illuminated various political, economic, social, and cultural anxieties. People, mostly youth, are taking to Iran's streets to express anger over the repression of the rights of national, religious, and sexual minorities, the increasing number of political prisoners, growing class differences, poverty, unemployment, environmental destruction, regional wars, the rise of refugees and migrants, in addition to the suppression of freedom of thought and expression. The upsurge of the uprising demonstrates how all forms of social *oppression,* whether based on sexuality or nationality, are interconnected with *exploitation,* that is, the class gap, poverty, homelessness, and unemployment. It also reflects the authoritarian-capitalist-theocratic nature of the Islamic regime. These *oppressive* and *exploitative* relations have been deeply ingrained within the fabric of society, and the state's religious ideology has legitimised and legalised these relationships according to Islamic law.

In considering this social and historical situation, the poets in this collection give us words to reflect on colossal events, from revolution and occupation to patriarchy, war poverty, and personal loss. Poems are the archive "to overcome fragilities of memories and erasure of histories."[4] Thus, the anthology explores the depths of human experience and reminds us that even in the face of adversity and atrocities, there is beauty, strength, and a profound connection to the genealogies of struggles, marked by intimate relationships and forbidden desires. The imagery of laughter, shadows, and unspoken confessions underscores the tension between sexual desires and the awareness of their potential power in confronting the self, society, sexuality, and the state. The poems invite readers to reflect on the interplay between past and present, the seen and the unseen, and the complex web of emotions that bind us to our histories and each other. The transformative power of poetry evokes a sense of displacement, longing, a call to wake up and search for understanding. Words like "knot", "suitcase", "liberty", "knife", "black bird", "mother's eyes", "letters", "path", "nemesis", "hands", along with abstract ideas, reveal deep emotional landscapes and a sense of unfinished revolutions that define our *jiyan/ life*. Let's return to the time, place, and the event: Jîna's Uprising.

On 16 September 2022, it was reported that Mahsa (Jîna) Amini, "a 22-year-old Iranian Kurdish woman, was arrested for improper veiling by the morality police and was brutally killed while in custody." In this one sentence, the sequencing of patriarchal, nationalist, theocratic state apparatus can be unpacked. First, the legalisation of gender apartheid in Iran's socio-cultural-political structure began on 8 March 1979, with subsequent laws in 1983, further criminalisation in the 1990s, followed by the establishment of the *Gasht-e Ershad* in 2005 which is multifariously called vice squad, Islamic Religious Police, morality police, or Guidance Patrol. In January 2018, there was a shift in the punishment for women accused of 'improper' veiling, particularly in Tehran. This shift is rooted in two circumstances of the rising number

4 Fereshte Moosavi (2024). "Archives as forms of resistance," *Journal of Visual Art Practice*, 23:1, 65-78.

of women violating the hijab law between 2014-2018 and the rise of protests throughout Iran. For example, in 2014, the Interior Minister reported that 220,000 women were taken to police stations to sign statements promising not to violate the hijab law. The Guidance Patrols, typically consisting of a van with a male crew and fully covered female officers, station themselves in busy public places to arrest women not adhering to government standards. Women are often violently slapped, beaten with batons, and pushed into police vans. On 27 December 2017, the head of the police in Tehran announced that those who do not observe Islamic values will no longer be taken to detention centres or courts but will instead be offered education classes to reform their behaviour. In these religious 're-education' centres, women must sign a form pledging not to commit the bad *hijabi* offense again and will receive police-organised guidance on how to observe Islamic values. Since 2009, social unrest and protests by women, workers, students, teachers, nurses, doctors, writers, environmentalists, and peace activists have occurred throughout the country over issues like unemployment, poverty, high fuel prices, inflation, and the hardships of sanctions, which have disproportionately benefited the ruling classes and their cronies. Significant other protest moments include: 2017-2018 Economic Protests; Girls of Revolution Street spontaneous acts of defiance; 2019 Price Hike Protests; and 11 January 2020 protests following the shooting down of Ukraine International Airlines Flight 752.

Second, there is the national question symbolised by her name. Let's explore the implication of naming: Mahsa (Jîna) Amini. A name that was parenthesised, (Jîna), to erase nationality and its long-standing resistance. Kurds have historically been denied the right to give Kurdish names to their children, often using two names – a Kurdish name at home and an administrative name for purposes like school registration and applying for civil servant jobs. Kurdish feminist scholars argue that the erasure of Jîna's Kurdish name and identity, along with dismissing the likely connection between her Kurdishness and the fatal state violence she experienced, reveals deeper patterns of erasure that Kurds have faced in modern Iran.[5] Rojhilatê is disproportionally suppressed economically and culturally. The entire region is a securitised and militarised zone. The state has targeted the Kurds with policies aimed at language and cultural assimilation. Although Kurds make up 10 per cent of the population, they represent 45 per cent of political prisoners in Iran. According to the Hengaw Organization for Human Rights, at least 266 prisoners were executed across Iran during the first half of 2024, among them 72 Kurds. The magnitude of violence and the myriad methods employed to bring pain and suffering on people are unparalleled in recent years. The state acts as an execution machine, and society ensnared in an immense machinery of violence. The ultimate aim of this brutality is to embed a culture of fear and intimidation, suppress all protests, and quell the flames of Jin, Jiyan, Azadi. Except that this powerful collection of poems accounts for a differing reality; the genuineness of a harrowing tale of resistance and sacrifice. They give us a vivid and evocative imagery to breathe freedom, democracy, and equality. The poems are a reminder of a powerful image of collective action. They underscore the strength found in solidarity and the unyielding human spirit. They capture the immense personal grief and collective struggle in Iran and Afghanistan over the last four decades. They serve as a stark reminder of the human cost of revolution, yet also embody relentless hope for change. The imagery of rivers, roads, trees, creeks, flowers, mountains, stones, and homes

5 Farangis Ghaderi and Ozlem Goner (2022). "Why 'Jîna': Erasure of Kurdish Women and Their Politics from the Uprisings in Iran," *Jadaliyya* (www.jadaliyya.com).

powerfully symbolises the continuity, meandering, exhaustion, and depletion experienced by women and society alike. The fragmented lines of the poems mirror the disjointed and chaotic nature of life and struggle during times of profound political, cultural, and social violence. Despite the overwhelming challenges and pervasive sense of loss, there is an underlying current of hope and determination. The poems invite readers to reflect on their own roles in the face of adversity and to consider the ways in which personal and collective struggles are intertwined. Just as Jîna's death became a 'secret/code' name and identity for a movement that represents both continuity and renewal of life and resistance,[6] *Jin, Jiyan, Azadi* is about remembering the inescapable shadows of past atrocities; it is a journey of remembrance and survival, from the horrors witnessed by previous generations to the introspective questioning of the new generation and our collective place in the world.

This anthology is a poetic rendition of a feminist movement centred on *life* and *freedom*. Each poem in this collection invites readers to witness the raw and unfiltered experiences of those who confront unimaginable hardship. Through the poet's masterful use of imagery and narrative, we are reminded of the enduring quest for freedom, justice, and dignity in the face of relentless adversity. As I pen these final words, women in prisons in Iran continue to send us recordings of their voices from behind the bars, crying out for freedom of all political prisoners and an end to the execution of women. Palestinians are fighting to gain peace, freedom, and 'home'. Indigenous People across the world are resisting the extractivist practices. All of these struggles capture the essence of resilience and the enduring revolutionary dreams.

---

6 Farangis Ghaderi Ghaderi (2024). "Jin, Jiyan, Azadi and the Historical Erasure of the Kurds." Roundtable: Woman, Life, Freedom: Reflections on an Enduring Crisis. International Journal of Middle East Studies 55 (4): 1–6.

Despite the overwhelming challenges and the pervasive presence of suppression, they send us messages of hope and determination. Their chants demanding *freedom* invites us to reflect on our own roles in collective struggles. As I read the poems in this anthology, the words and voices of those who resist and insist on peace, freedom and democracy, resonate in my mind and heart.

Shahrzad Mojab
Professor of Women and Gender Studies
University of Toronto

"*Songs Of Freedom* is an important book, an anthology of poetry by ten Iranian and Afghan women poets writing in the face of violent repression and forced exile. Every page resonates with anger and love, with the sense that love will win out in the end, with the justified craving for natural freedoms and the huge struggles against institutional social and personal violence. That this is a book of women's voices matters the most and it is vital for us to hear what is being said: yes, ten different voices across the individual poets, but more overwhelmingly, their shared voice of absolute tenacity and the courage of their lyric struggle. Many thanks to the publisher Afsana Press, and above all to the ten poets who are giving us their work, mostly translated from Farsi, so that we can hear them now in English and thus better understand how and why their freedom songs are so important and matter so much."
–**Stephen Watts**, poet and translator, author of *Republic of Dogs/ Republic of Birds*

Azita Ghahreman

Azita is a writer and poet, born in Mashhad, Iran. She has published six collections of poetry in Farsi, and three collections and two stories in Swedish. Her first poetry book, *Eve's Songs*, was published in 1990. Her poems have been translated into many languages, including German, French, Turkish, Arabic, Hindi, Russian, Spanish and Italian. A collection of her poetry, *Negative of a Group Photograph* (Bloodaxe Books 2018), won an English Pen award, and a selection of her poems in Russian and Ukrainian was awarded the "Little Ludwig Noble Prize" in 2014 by the Udmurtia Russian Academy. Azita's work has been reviewed in the literary world. On several occasions, she has been a judge for the young poets' contest at the Jaleh Esfahani Cultural Foundation. Her last collection of stories, *Somewhere to Get Lost,* was published in Sweden in 2022.

Azita's poem in this book is translated from Farsi by Rouhi Shafii.

My Mother's Eyes

My mother's eyes, a rainbow,
and a phoenix that hid in the sky,
brought me to the earth.
In a tight nest, I grew wings and feathers.
Crows stole my umbilical cord.
Tied wishes to the branch of Tuba,[7]
my aunt, who knew poetry, nursed me.
In the year of turmoil, she was quietly killed,
in a mansion with high walls.
But she bequeathed:
Do not forget the cypresses in the garden,
and keep the words warm in your chest.

After her, with the grandmother's tales,
a thousand fairies and a magic bird
were tamed in my stammering tongue.

With a needle of tears and black thread,
she wrote a notebook,
full of red flowers and dawn.
Every night, a candle was lit,
and on foot, we returned from the mountain and ridge,
to meet that lost beloved.

To sketch the holes and fallen pieces,

7 The name of a mythological tree in the Persian tales.

I, who did not know embroidery,
covered the torn seams with the alphabet.
A salve and a cry, for the rope around Talat's throat,
the wounds on Rana's chest,
the cracks in every corner.
But poetry is a set of nested mirrors,
letters of cracked corners,
which become loud sobs with no owner.

Perhaps the alphabet does not understand the heart,
but the view of every sunny field
reminds me of your warm face.

Even after the age of seven,
as I ran towards solitude,
and got lost in the hustle of
the Farsi homework and arithmetic lessons,
life was hectic.
Other mothers came.
They wrote my name for adoption,
and entrusted me to fate.

O, jealous tree by the cemetery corner,
you were right.
Only in dreams, wakefulness shapes into reality.
Rivers flow toward the sea.
We fly like birds,
and like freedom,
we are dear and beautiful.

Chasing the flickering of that star,
in the year of revolution,
an eccentric mother,
combed my dishevelled hair,
tied a red ribbon,
and we fled, ran toward the valley,
with broken hands and feet,
and closed eyes.
Which dream were you seeking,
inside the burnt books?

We observed the city in this way,
understood people thus,
in the Wednesday market of the world's stammer,
the old windows returned, to decorate our Eid.

After the war, famine came.
No embrace, no love letter, no kiss.
Bitter and mad,
I walked step by step with death on the alleyway,
and returned to poetry with black tulips.

Where the gates of heaven and hell
had a twisted design,
the demon's profile next to Farrokhlagha's[8] face,
on the market's humid ceiling,
a pomegranate feast and sweet kisses,

8 Farrokhlagha means a beautiful woman

banners and adorned maces raised,
malevolent spirits and the scent of cauldrons of offerings,
for the supper of the seven-headed dragon.

A song from Ghamar,[9]
a verse full of love from Qurratulain,[10]
a poem from Forough[11] brought a miracle,
suddenly, the sun became bright,
perhaps the truth was in those two young green hands,
those two young green hands…

Where the eyes do not see each other in blindness,
no hand holds another, in the midst of the frost,
poetry is the hooting of a strange line,
the narrators wrote in the air,
with glowing letters,
and shining dots.

Now the absentees speak with your mouth,
with lips that still throb under the soil,
in love and bruised.

The mother you never saw,
at the corner of a deserted place,
hidden from all,
brought you a sister,

9 Ghamar was the first Iranian woman singer

10 Tahereh Ghoratalein, A scholar of Islamic and Bahai faith and the first woman who took off her veil in public 200 years ago.

11 Forough Farakhzad, a bold, feminist, poet of the 20th century Iran.

you should have sought all your life
to find her,
among the dead, the lovers,
the hungry and the lonely.

In the grand tapestry of the homeland,
did you not see her,
with black hair, with torn canvas shoes?
Those days when the school master,
made a ritual of burying bloody clothes,
and tying off severed veins?

Silence is another name for fear,
or disgust.
Silence that casts a shadow over terror.
Disgust that cast a shadow on a frozen smile,
on the morning of the first day of Farvardin,
when the cherry blossoms bloomed,
and the doves cried out on the stone.

I looked.
There, it was the carpet market.
Here, was the turquoise crossroads.
The prayer hall and the flickering candles,
a cold breeze from an unseen window,
a twisting shadow called my name.

They say, the soul has vast and winding expanses,
and on human skin is an unreadable map,

from the journey's path towards the sea.

Wish, they would plant me
in another land anew,
so, I bear fruit with the taste of apple.
But for stealing a secret
from a forbidden book,
they punished me to carve 'farewell,'
a hundred times on the prison wall
It's a simple confession,
instead of conquering the world with passion and fervour,
we just mothered,
burned and built from the ashes.
A story that joined water and the wind.
Hope is just this!

Years passed.
Will one day, my mother find my stone?
Recognise my picture in an old newspaper,
buy me a wedding dress?

I leave all these,
beside the unfinished sentences,
and the long corridors of the metro,
a forest covered with dew and frost,
a wild bird that cries out at midnight,
and knows our language.

The dogs, the official letters, and the tax papers,

snow-covered railings,
and signs for the hearing-impaired,
on the river path,
are always there.

I ask you, grandmother,
how should I arrange all these,
so as to narrate today and the bygones,
to record our yesterdays' promises and agreements,
without disappearing,
the sun that you bequeathed to us as a keepsake?

I know a long labyrinth is still ahead.
All my mothers in the stories
are scattered and nameless.
Sometimes by dialling a number,
you can watch their voices from afar,
like an invisible wave on white paper.
But many unknown girls have appeared,
in my dreams every night.
They swore by all that is light and joy and salt
that they will soon come into the world.
I am waiting for them.
Awaiting them to be reborn me anew.

Ava Homa

Ava Homa is an acclaimed author, speaker, and faculty member at California State University, Monterey Bay. Her debut novel, *Daughters of Smoke and Fire* (HarperCollins & Abrams, 2020), was named one of the best books of the year by the *Wall Street Journal* (US), the *Independent* (UK), and *Globe and Mail* (Canada). It was featured in Roxane Gay's Book Club, won the 2020 Nautilus Silver Book Award for Fiction, and was a finalist for the 2022 William Saroyan International Writing Prize. Her short story collection, *Echoes from the Other Land,* was nominated for the 2011 Frank O'Connor Short Story Prize. Ava holds a master's degree in English and Creative Writing from the University of Windsor, and her essays and fiction have been published and anthologized in the UK, US, and Canada. She has delivered speeches across Europe and North America, including at the United Nations in Geneva.

Liberté, Égalité, Sororité

Your flowing hair is a noose
constricting my heart, beloved, he whispered.
If it dances freely in the breeze,
my life shall dissipate with the wind.
I let him cloak me,
for love.

Your unveiled tresses kindle divine wrath,
the clergy declared
Your locks, before prying eyes,
shall shake the earth with tremors,
the sky with tempests.
A black scarf concealed all my colours,
for God.

Your exposed hair is a plot of imperialists,
comrades accused,
When unbound, the nation shall be betrayed,
your brethren stabbed in the back,
solidarity brutalized.
Deaf to my pleas, they veiled me,
for the laws.

Shrouded and disappearing, I sang
a song
fingers gripping the bars,

curls drenched in sweat and disguised.
Yet they demonized my voice,
criminalized my every word.
Virtuous girls are inconspicuous, they howled.

Pressed against a lonely wall,
I caught a woman's lullabies,
muffled, I hummed along
mourning our alienation,
grieving beauties vilified
wanting liberty, wanting life.

Slowly a chorus joined in.
Crescendoing, our voices shattered stalls.
Storming outside, we set our veils ablaze
twirling around flames that
devoured headscarves and our frights.

Boots marched in and handcuffed us
our vocal cords
twitching
as coerced confessions were televised.

Still, we rose,
heads held high,
hair floating in the wind,

passing on the torch of Kurdish defiance
chanting *Jin-Jiyan-Azadi*

the Woman, Life, Freedom slogan
transcending the fallen,
raising the torch that shall illuminate
the tunnel out of which we crawl.

For a Fledgling Revolution

She's dying &
you're protesting &
a crimson river is bending.

He's dying & the is dying may end now
or a week from now
or in a few years
& the river is tired of bending.

She's dying &
you leave him with the pain &
you take away your painkilling presence
to march on the streets.

He's dying & you chant death to the dictator &
death to sanctions that took away his medications &
death to the hefty bills that resulted from
your attempts at interrupting
the is dying.

She's dying
& you're working
& you're dying
& she's working on not dying,
and the river is
drying.

My Wilderness

… we cannot be friends
not in the land of our birth,
nor in the desert of exile
        Oh exile exile
        a punishment disguised as a prize
        a withering in the fringes
        of a not-your-country
where I carry the upturned earth
and torn roots in my palms.

We cannot be friends
not when desire masquerades as tenderness
the line blurs and I capsize
        home was rainforest for your people
        and relentless draught for mine
        and still the scent of your hands
        reminds me of the jasmine
        Grandpa planted in my hair.

We cannot be friends
not when the highs of fleeting
togetherness is followed by brutal lows
        you don't hear
        the dry leaves crunching under our feet
        you don't feel
        the rough texture of the barks.

We cannot be friends
not when the abrupt pangs of
longing make my words gag and
writhe

you remain oblivious and
I yearn for Father's goodbye kiss upon my forehead
for the lips of a first love upon mine…

The Golden Bees of Kurdistan

I hail from the land of crown lilies and
genocide and retch every time boots
stain the lilies with blood.

I settle beside a creek and commemorate
uncles planted into a mass grave.
Grandma's windows shattered. She

ran out and jumped over the corpses
of her siblings and neighbors.
She transmuted into a seed, buried beside her sons.

I traverse unforgiving terrains, past
slumbering serpents and vibrant
butterflies. Feet kissing the Earth

with each step, I whisper, who is this *I*?
And since the killer and we are all called humans,
what does *we* signify?

I settle beside a creek, absorbed by the golden bees
toiling on pink and white flowers, oblivious
to their symphony and rainbow

to their vital part in the cascade of life.
Suddenly – tenderly – a mist descends

upon my chest, a whisper, *You're*

much like those bees, unaware.
I plunge into the ocean's depth, awed
by the dancing coral reef, underappreciated

by colour-blind sea life. Asking the unanswerable, I
whisper who are the reefs splendid for?
For whom does the ocean beautify?

Nemesis

Your laughter dissolves
in my grip
in my grief

in the furnace of abstinence
we melt away
we don't confess

like when I step into
your shadow and
play ambivalent

or when your breath whispers
through my hair and
you play innocent

when I memorize the sound of
your sturdy footsteps and you
the perfume on my neck

your terrifying eyes
pull me in, the rip current I
can't deny

my lips on yours
taste like a crime
we wouldn't survive

Cremation

I watch you fade under the moonlight, transforming
into a distant star, and where it hurts in my body is
the hollow on the right side of my chest, where
my heart would be if it were on the right, where
the myth says 'the spiritual heart' resides.

To you, I bow, you were the one who
took me across the milky galaxy. I
twirled in my space suit to witness
the vastness of freedom & love.

As you billow out, so flies with you
the parts of me glued to your eyes—nay, that's wrong,
so departs with you all the particles of me that
cry for you, to every inch that I've kissed, that is to say,
to all of you, but mostly accompanying your eyes. When closed,
they carry the imprint of my lips.

The distance will stretch my being, reaching
across planets to caress your face
one last time.
We were in a tango, a dance
near and far, and as we played hide and seek or
ascended high and sank low on a seesaw, a cavity
in my soul filled and spilled over. A metamorphosis,
magical, illogical. This poem unlocks passion
only in the sanctuary of loss.

I perished in my dream last night,
submerged in the ocean, I fractured, lower body
carried away, torso dangling upside down, each
segment gliding in a direction. You
solemnly witnessed my disintegration. Surprised,
I smiled. *Hey, I'm alive*. Dissolution somehow
wasn't the end, but the beginning of holding
death in my broken arms.

Ziba Karbassi

Ziba Karbasi was born in Tabriz, north-western Iran, and has lived in the UK since her teenage years. Her first book in Farsi was published in her early twenties. Since then, she has published twelve poetry collections in both Farsi and other languages. These include her trilingual book, *Ooooooommm* (Mille Gru, 2011) and *Collage Poems* (Exiled Writers Ink, 2009). Her work has been translated into more than fifteen languages. She is widely regarded as one of the leading poets of her generation living in exile. She is known for her dense, revolutionary and lyric poetry, and has performed her poems widely across Europe and America. In 1997, she introduced a subject to poetry known as Breath Poetry. In 2009, she won the Golden Apple Poetry Price in Azerbaijan. In 2012, she was chosen by the Contemporary Poetics Research Centre (CPRC), Birkbeck, University of London, as a writer whose language epitomises the revolutionary power of poetry when faced by the crises of our lives in the contemporary world. Ziba was chairperson of the Iranian Writers Association (in exile) from 2002 to 2004, and chair of Exiled Writers Ink in the UK from 2012 to 2014. She has served as a director of PEN international relations (Iran in exile) from 2019 to the beginning of 2021.

Ziba's peoms in this book are translated from Farsi by Nazlee Radboy.

1

For Tomaj Salehi

I have bitten off the star on your sport shoes
With my canine teeth
My mouth is red with blood
Come back

2

I'm ashamed and disgraced by this cryptic language
It turns you into a clown
When the bricks of prison
Have crumbled from your blood

2
Letter 346 B

Know me from your knowing
Your knowledge
Understand me from your understanding
Your understood
Your nature
Not from the frame of intellect
But from the subconscious of your subconscious
Not from your library
But from the bare bones of its ink
That personal
That distinctive
That exclusive
Your genuine
Your genius
Your spherical volume of trust
Unshackling outside
Uncorrupted inside
If this is humanity
Don't be human
Love in a way
That your greatest response to treachery
Is to be detached

3
Letter 400 A

We come from worth
And reached Worthy
To rejoin uncovers
The spherical bokeh
On the horizon line
In vertical view
Whatever starts from Zero
Never ends at Zero
I have lived in such a way
It seems there is no tomorrow
Follow the lines of joy on walls of ancient caves and start to dance
Beauty has ruled me Yusuf
The moon has become my ruler
To die is something
But
Not to die is more thing
Oh
Those who live on love
On which thick finger tip are you sitting
From merciful compassion
My baby was born
Called a poem
I am not the kind of mother
Who lets the stairway surpass my child

4

Nooooof
No
You cannot
Under no condition
In no way possible
Not in any dimension of existence
Divert or distract me
From my path
If you are so sure of yourself
If you're telling the truth
Tell me
Til' now
How many times have you died
For a poem

5
Letter 51

In the yearning air
Affection was slow
When night blooming-jasmines
Lost their scent
Senseless
The pillow next to me
Fluffed for no reason
with an embrace that sized up the moon
From the path of wolves
You have come
Until dusk
You merely sampled my deer flesh
And resisted
Fresh bite marks on skin
In fact
You came from the path of wolves
Returned a buck
But
Left your horns
Inside me
Without a trace

6
Closer than Sigh 17

If you're scared
What are you scared of
If you love me
After what do you love me
If you really want
Everything will take the shape
Of a heart
Even a gravestone

7
Letter 28

Love knows no rationale in its path
Madness cannot justify its own psychosis
Love has shattered me into a million pieces
I am the steadiness of turtles' tracks
Behind my madness, sharp understanding
Stuntedness of flowers' throat
The silence of the whiteness in a buttock of snow
The still tongue of my speechlessness
I am not ha ha ha
Or
ho ho ho
Drowned in tears
Soreness of muscles
The whistling of bones
Out-of-sight ceiling
Not a wall
Four columns
Not a frame
But the foundation
Bite on my liver guts
Gun powder
Trigger
Barrel
The anticipation of my scabbard

Don’t devalue value
You can count on me
Don’t close the book

8
Letter 381 A

The mother of a child
Whose woollen silk cardigan looked like a splash of rainbow
Was pushing a buggy
and with every shake and bump
From her blessed breast
Leaked hot milk
The flower-patterned napkin
Under her sutian was moistening
Oh you
Kinder than mothers soft warm milk
In the mouth of a hungry child
Truer
Pleasanter
More lovable than the tin rays of light
On the shoulder of stained glasses
In the temple of the body
In the time of hot romancing
The vibe of grandfathers raised eyebrow
Heavy
Thick and tall
From the veins dignity bashfulness
Oh
The only small difference
Between human and machine
In the size of heart

9
For Poem

I am also a dog of this word
It has attached a collar around my neck
It leaves me wet under the rain
I jump up impulsively
I wag my tail
In wake
I dream of fluffy cotton clouds
They climb over top of me
Boom
Boom
They fart and laugh
In an unconscious state
I see the word
Whose eyelids don't shut for one moment
That boils from the depths of the water
Like a dark pit
It buzzes around
It comes up
Takes air
And while under its wings fill with the breeze
It pours colour in to abstract multi-dimensional shapes
Within vibrant toys
Natural instance
From all of this
A single bone
Thrown before me

10

For Sepideh Gholian*

1

Let the bars of prison whisper in each other's ear
showing off their iron biceps
with smug gestures
we hide our tears
behind laughter
Your name passes
through the keyhole.

2

Your drapes are red with blood Sepideh
Underneath your name
Many stars have broken.

* Sepideh means dawn in Farsi.

Note: For the past fifteen years, Ziba has been writing thirty volumes of a long poetry novel in the form of letters, titled *Letters of Bahador Dorrani and Ahoo Hessani*. Some of the poems are included in this book.

Soheila Mirzaei

Soheila Mirzaei was born in Urmia in north-west Iran. She spent her childhood in Azerbaijan before migrating with her family to Tehran. She has been passionate about literature and writing poetry since her teenage years. In the 1970s, she participated in poetry and storytelling workshops led by the acclaimed Iranian novelist, poet and critic, Reza Baraheni. Soheila's first book was published during this period, coinciding with her migration to Germany. Her books include *I slip From My Hands,* (Aida Publications, Germany, 2013); *Diaspora of Poetry,* an anthology of poetry by modern Iranian women (Aftab Publications, Norway, 2021); *Elmiden Doshurum,* a bilingual poetry collection in Farsi and Azeri; *Michka Sings Illegally* (Mortazavi Publications, Germany, 2005); and *I Remain with a Sin* (Hamgam Publications, Tehran, Iran, 1998).

Soheila's peoms in this book are translated from Farsi by Rouhi Shafii.

1

S

I was a sigh that my mother let out.
I began with a dot,
at the start of a line.
As soon as I stood on my feet,
I set forth on my path.
Became audacious.
Ignored big mouths.
They smelled of naphthalene inside my grandmother's shroud.

My body, allergic to some words:
Judge, law, bolt and contract.
I let my thighs live.
Crossed the boundary of the body to reach the self.
If you reach the middle of the road,
you will slide down.

Keep your head high.
Your body straight.
Now, you are standing on the pages.
Dance, ballet dance.
Flap your wings.
Flap.

G

It is grown up, I have to grow up.

I am indifferent to the worms in the computer,
even if snakes replace them.
If I have gone further than my feet,
and my brain has ordered,
by the side of this dry brook,
I will lie down.
Now, let the newspapers cry your name.
Big, or small,
in whatever corner,
what difference does it make?

2

Perhaps you are a naked prostitute,
in the labyrinth of a lecherous gaze,
its cheapness sickens the hearts.

Perhaps a girl wears her red dress,
with that a marigold petal upon her hair,
thinking of a bitter traveller,
who will never reach destination.

3

I am a woman resembling a trapezius,
multiplying and ever multiplying.
One corner of me takes refuge in your secret deeds.
Another, returning from a night's flirt,
and the other isolates itself at a corner,
always wanting to say I am pointless, you are pointless.

Another corner of mine laughs heartily
and says don't think about it!
The other, a little further away
stands upright and keeps saying,
it's late, hurry up

And I swallow in panic,
I swallow everything.

My corners that are so much like me
are not always the corners of a trapezoid.
Sometimes I remain a square,
and suffocate in that four-walled room.
When my corners pick on each other,
I vomit.
And my heart trembles for my helplessness!

Her Throat Was Filled with the Street

I dance fire, my face with my hair, my hair, my hair
From the hair, the throat
The street dances the pine tree.

The street filled with raw dreams.
Bunches, bunches, streets,
I became blood, red as a fish.

Until they turn into dust
I turn into blood,
as a fish.
Until they turn into dust
I turn into blood,
so they turn into dust.
I turn blood, dry
Become blood on the wall.

Poison
The taste of my mother's mouth.
The grave, the scaffolding becomes the hanging stand.
Had they given his medication?
His dream, his dream!
Your hair
A rope round the neck.
What plans do they pour down the throat to the neck!
Love has another duty now!

Love has another duty now!
My kisses
My kisses are looking for your neck.
For you, my romantic poems
For you, the godless of beauty!

The Wall

(In Memory of Mohammad Mokhtari, Mohammad Jafar Pooyandeh, and …) In the most barren winter of the city, I became pregnant in the companion of the walls and letters. I would eat the words, talk to the wall, became the wall, and my poem would crack. I played love games with the neighbour's wall! The eyes of the bricks were dizzy and in love with me. Pain struck me from behind, into my mouth. In my morning sickness, I vomited words. My poem wept!

A poem stretched across the floor,
thrown into the air, hammered into the ground.
Letters cast shadows upon the city.
The night watchmen are with me,
and away from me, moved away from me,
are with me.
Images orbit the wall,
speak, transform – perhaps into poetry.
Space for poetry has become narrow.
Push the city walls, push them. Push them.
Blows upon my head. I have become love.
Some beloved guests behind the door,
Fluid letters in the air,
They make love with me, I am on fire from the winter's fire.
I carry a child in my belly.
My morning sickness, the wall.
My head, heavy, my sky poetry.
Press my stomach, twist me against the wall, spin me round the city.
Spin me, knock me down,
perhaps my poem will cry fervently.

The Path

I am a suitcase.
Travelling from this city to that.
Enduring train delays.
The rain that lifts from my feet.
A hand that clutches my throat.
We have stopped behind the shadows.

Voices pour out of my head.
You settle in my body.
Cities, villages, rivers, and mountains
shout that we simplified you.
Years fall upon the flowers of my dress.
Their creases rise above my age.

I am locked with a code you have forgotten.
I am a suitcase.
Full of the twists and turns of the passersby.
Full of the glasses that have shattered in my eyes.

The scent of silence has dampened me.
Even with delays, trains do not reach their destination.
I promise,
before I run in my sleep and do not arrive,
I will wake up behind the narrator's eyelids.

The Knot

Lift your finger.
There's an itch in my throat where a stroke looms.
Take away your cough.
So, I may become thin in the heart of this alleyway.

The rope does not have the strength for this length.
Should the stool drop,
I will become past tense until later.

The hand of my clock knows my conditions
even
when your ring has swallowed my finger.

From which Spot Did It Happen?

From which spot in my head does it fall
when they turn naked among the pieces of the dress?
From which spot in my head had it passed,
as the cold droplets returned to the depth of my eyes?
As the word was no God but a thorn.

I should remember to water the base of every word,
and draw a tree,
to be a safe place for the letters,
as they slide out of your head.

Close to My Body

To my master Reza Baraheni, and in memory of our poetry and our stories workshop in that basement, which was a gateway to serious poetry.

Shadows have emptied
on the first line of the wall
Chewing and munching, over the stomach's kneading
I am cleansed up to the hollow of the mouth
My mirror is stained
No matter how much I clean it,
the stains turn into finger.

– The eyes have betrayed their sockets
Close the door, this season has an irritating rustle

My head under the skies of my land, my soil
anddddd my fist,
a fistful of the sky!
– I snatched it savagely –

Your head is underwater, no matter half a foot, or a foot deep.
At night, my shoes walk without me.
They spin so I don't fall.
They laugh as I grind my teeth.
They sit down, I set off.
Even if books fall from my head word by word,
or shadows leave my head

You've stitched your stains onto my skirt,
scrub and rub,
stay piece by piece.
It has heavy hands this needle.

Stone

From among the hands which all look alike,
black.
From among the stones which are of the same grain,
big and small,
a stoney mouth insults
you and me.
On the chalky white behind the frame,
it has turned into ash.
Ahead of you, under this blue ceiling
under this heaviness which holds you,
I am standing.
Your gaze under a pile of stone
has turned into sunset.
And under this blue ceiling,
I raise my skirt,
so that you can rise again.

Sana Nassari

Born in 1985, Sana Nassari is a young award-winning Iranian writer, poet, and literary translator, based in London. To date she has published one novel of her own, and translated four novels by the American multi-award-wining writer Karen Joy Fowler, and a novel by the late Polish writer Marek Hłasko, into Farsi. A chapbook of Sana's short stories, *These Two Roses,* has been published by Exiled Writers Ink (London, 2020). Her debut poetry collection, *Departure*, has been published by the reputable publishing house Morvarid in Iran. Also, her poetry collection, *Oh Delilah,* was due to be published by Morvarid, but was banned by the country's censor authorities. This collection won the second prize for unpublished collections from the Journalists' Poetry Award. Sana has recently obtained an MA in History of Art at SOAS, University of London. Currently, she writes reviews and essays for the *Writers Mosaic* magazine.

In the Canebrake

I walk in the canebrake
The day is gradually getting short
I feel time is running away

I walk in the canebrake
I feel these small scratches
Make me prettier

I walk
And whisper a poem
That I have never read.

I do not speak about you
The wind makes the reeds whine
Without any reason.

The Death Foretold

Every step that I took
brought me closer to the city I was escaping from
the sound of knife rose from my bones
I wanted to cover myself
but the sand
only mirrored my feet in itself and kept retreating
I remembered
the Arab woman called me
in a busy market.
She had read my palm from the distance
Your future is a book of a thousand leaves, she said.
Where one sentence is repeated time and again.
But I can't read
the letters
the alphabet, she said
and disappeared into the crowd
rushing towards vegetables, yoghurts, and dates.
Beware!
Her voice came from a distance
Know and beware!
that these people can't bear
the sad beauty of young women
become either old
or hidden, she said.
Neither was possible.

Translated from Farsi by Alireza Abiz.

Morning Routine

You turn the same key in the lock
You whisper the same song
You pass through the same corridor
The same stove
The same tea
The same book on the table
The same sound of my breathing while asleep
The same semi-dark room
Nothing has changed
Only I am not
In this house anymore.

Circular

He was a sailor
And added insult to his wife's injury every night
To her
He didn't talk about the seas
He didn't talk about the waves
To her
He didn't talk about the rivers
He didn't talk about the fishing nets.
To her
He didn't talk about
The cities faraway
The migrating birds

The woman
Was alone
She had never gone on any trips
But she knew that in this world
There are other women
That have never gone on any trips
But they knew that
There are
Other women.

Stoning

Then we cursed them in Arabic
تراب القُبور عَليكُم *
and everything turned into stone
the massive hands of our dads
the flaming rage of the strangers
the air
our tears
and the hole in which we were buried.

* May the dust of the graves be upon you

Liberty

I write: Liberty
It cannot stay a word
It goes, becomes a tower
It goes, casts its shadow on the sleep of the unemployed workers
It goes, beautifies the sunset behind it
It goes, takes souvenir photos with passengers , with taxi drivers
It goes to the crowd and colludes with people
Up in arms
Chanting slogans
It goes to the jail
And never returns to this crumpled paper again.

Like a Knife upon Itself

Like a knife
In the moment of blood burst

Like a knife
Whose shining blade could
Repeat the image of a beautiful woman's lips
In its red blood memory
But didn't

Like a knife
That could have sliced bitter oranges
But slipped
On the pale joints

Like a knife
In the flank of a man who had no role in my misery

Like a knife
Like a handle of a knife
That every time
A hand touched it
It trembled
And couldn't delay a punishment

Like a knife from behind
From the side

Like a knife
That in the moment of blood burst
Is cold but remorseful
I wept within myself
Yet no one realised.

The Last Floor

We step into an old apartment
With brown parquet floors
A spacious hall
An old piano covered in dust
A kitchen adorned with green cabinets
My mother opens a door
Everything is extraordinarily beautiful
She shuts the door
And her voice fades away
The wardrobe
Is vast and deep
With a small window at the end
Overlooking a hidden garden
Where each time she's there
My mother catches a whiff of a small flower.

Jarrahi*

In childhood,
I used to run in its canebrake
It was beautiful
My hands would graze against it
I didn't know a small wound
could remain open forever.

In childhood,
I smelled the green box trees of its houses
People passed by, happily
Blood flowed in veins
Not in streets.

In the small Jarrahi market,
a man was holding his son's hand
The boy was beautiful
And no bullet
ever crossed his forehead.

In childhood,
in the alleys, we'd run
We wouldn't flee from anyone.

In childhood,
I swam in the Jarrahi river
The blood was the same colour as water

We didn't know

it couldn't be washed away from the body.

* A reference to the Mahshahr, Jarrahi Massacre – the mass killing of protesters in the Iranian city of Mahshahr in November 2019, during the 2019–2020 protests in Iran.

In Your Realm

In vain, amidst the desert of words
In search of you,
I exhausted myself
You: an invisible ruler
Encompassing everything
At night
Cloaked in a decaying robe
You came to the desert as a shepherd
Your wooden cane
Sliding over sands
You transformed me into a bird
I rose to flee
Only to collide with glass
Transparent glass, an hourglass.

"*Songs of Freedom*, an anthology written by Iranian and Afghan women poets, is both a literary work and a song of protest. As the PEN Women's Manifesto states: 'Across the globe, culture, religion and tradition are repeatedly valued above human rights and are used as arguments to encourage or defend harm against women and girls. PEN believes that the act of silencing a person is to deny their existence. It is a kind of death. Humanity is both wanting and bereft without the full and free expression of women's creativity and knowledge.' I celebrate these pages that honour the intelligence, individuality and creativity of Iranian and Afghan poets who also speak for their silenced sisters."

–**Jennifer Clement**, poet, novelist and President Emerita of PEN International, author of *Prayers for the Stolen*

Nasrin Parvaz

Nasrin Parvaz became a civil rights activist when the Islamic regime took power in 1979. She was arrested in 1982, tortured and spent eight years in prison. Her books include *One Woman's Struggles in Iran: a prison memoir* (award-winner in the Women's Issues category of 2019 International Book Awards), and *The Secret Letters from X to A* (Victorina Press, 2018). Her prison memoir has also been published in Spanish and German. Her new novel, *Coffee*, was longlisted for Bath Novel Award 2023. Some of Nasrin's short stories and poems have been published in various anthologies. She has also translated poems into English and published a novel in Farsi about the massacre of prisoners in 1988 in Iran, to which she was an eyewitness. Nasrin has written articles in national newspapers. She is a regular participant in discussion panels and has been frequently interviewed about the situation in Iran on national radio and TV. Her paintings have been in various exhibitions, and on postcards and calendars. Nasrin studied for a degree in psychology and subsequently gained an MA in International Relations. She then completed a Postgraduate Diploma in Applied Systemic Theory at the Tavistock and Portman NHS Foundation Trust, where she worked in a team of family therapists for some time.

Woman, Life, Freedom

Shot, handcuffed to the flag rod.
He asked for water
the guards held a cup of water
out of reach and said, *Take it.*

His mother came at dawn
with a bowl of water.
She was shot.

His sister came
with a bowl of water.
She was shot.

His cousin came
with a bowl of water.
She was shot.

His neighbour came
with a bowl of water.
She was shot.

His lover came at dusk
together with women.
Each holding a bowl of water.

Frightened
the guards ran away.

Published in: *Ourselves in Rivers and Oceans: A poetry anthology* (Wee Sparrow Poetry Press, 2024)

Black Bird

Which of these thousands
of standing stones
engraved with a black number
belongs to you?
Stones
as white as a bride's dress
you never wore.
You were a black bird
caught by men
your father
or brother
who plucked your feathers
one
by
one
throughout your life
before
slashing your throat.

Published in: *Welcome to Britain: An Anthology of Poems and Short Fiction* (Civic Leicester, 2023)

That Sunny Afternoon in Cyprus

The face of a man born
in a different part of the world
brings you to mind
I need to call your name
have you walk towards me
you were holding my hand
we were talking
I jolted violently
the sound of a gunshot
your hand slipped from mine
you bent
double
flattened
on the pavement
your red shirt turned black.

The Invader

Her small pretty face framed with black hair
shines like a gem on the shore
her fear glazed eyes are open
her parted lips dead blue.
The clear blue waters of the Mediterranean
wash the little invader.

Published in: *Over Land, Over Sea: poems for those seeking refuge* (Five Leaves Publications, 2015)

Dream

I wake up from
a difficult dream
and find out
there is no disease.
No one has died.
My friend who nursed me
in prison
has not been ill
for the last six months.

Life goes on
except after years
of suffocation
under grey smoke
the sky is blue
in Tehran again.

Published in: *Can you hear the people sing? Global responses to the pandemic* (Palewell Press, 2020)

The Last Time I Saw You

I was a few minutes early.
To kill time

I went to a phone box
and called a friend,

still watching the street
looking out for you.

I was laughing with her
when I saw you in the back of a car

with two hard-looking men.
Your right arm was in a sling.

I knew you'd seen me
but you looked

straight through me
and I knew I too

was in danger.
I turned away

my friend still chattering in my ear
but I no longer heard her,

my mind was full of you.
Out of the corner of my eye

I watched the car
going up and down the road

looking for me.

Published in: Finished Creatures Poetry Magazine (Spring 2022)

Acting

It must had been his first day of begging
he was clean and good looking
standing, rather than sitting
he took a step or two towards the passers by
smiling and asking politely for spare change.
I mistook him for George Clooney, acting
in one of his Hollywood films.

I imagined him afterwards
washing himself thoroughly
in one of his glass showers
in one of his mansions
that could house hundreds of beggars.

Published in: *Welcome to Britain: An Anthology of Poems and Short Fiction* (Civic Leicester, 2023)

Red on White

Holding her child's hand
pregnant, panicked
she looks for her ticket
in her bag.
The police
drag her onto the white platform
in a white country.
The child is frozen
lost behind boots
watching
the stream of blood
coming out
from between
her mother's legs.

Published in: *Alien edition anthology* (Fly on the Wall, December 2020)

Colnbrook Immigration Removal Centre

You wake up to the sound of
the first early morning plane
landing at Heathrow.
Then you go back to your dreams
thinking about the passengers in the plane
wondering if any of them are like you.
Traveling on a false passport.

Hazily you remember
that some rich man
has bought this prison
all the inmates included
just like serfs or slaves
and you try to figure out
how anyone makes money
holding you prisoner.

Published in: *Write to be Counted: An Anthology of Poetry to Uphold Human Rights* (The Book Mill, 2017)

Liberty!

In Freedom Square in Tehran
workers gather at sunrise
waiting to be picked up for a job.

Unwittingly they go to build a prison
where one day they will be locked up
for demanding their own rights.

Their only reward is a blindfold
but the jailers themselves cannot see
the workers
reading familiar walls with one hand
while the fingers of the other
are tapping out the Morse for Liberty.

Translated in collaboration with British Bilingual Poetry Collective (BBPC)
18.06.2023.

"*Songs of Freedom* is an important book representing the voices of exiled Iranian and Afghan women poets. As such it is a seminal work and a reminder of the need to speak out through poetry with precision on what matters most in our world. This anthology, appearing at a time of division and uncertainty, is a gift to poetry and our international poetry culture. The women here have found their voices and generously use them in positive and life affirming ways for a better world. There is so much to praise and admire."

–**David Caddy**, poet, critic and literary sociologist, author of *Interiors, and Other Poems*

Mehrangiz Rassapour (M. Pegah)

Mehrangiz Rassapour (M. Pegah) is a poet, literary critic, translator and editor of *Vajeh* (Word), a Persian cultural and literary magazine. Born in Khoram-Abad, in south-east Iran, she started writing poetry when she was nine and had her first ghazal published in a prestigious literary magazine when she was thirteen. Her first book of poetry, *Spark Dies At Once* (*Jaragheh Zood Mimirad*) was published in Iran in 1992, followed by her second collection *And Then the Sun* (*Va Sepass Aftaab*) in the UK, then *Birds are Out of Date* (*Parandeh Digar, Na*), published in Germany. Her fourth book, *The Planet of Pause* (*Sayaareh Ye Derang*) was published in April 2012. Her critically acclaimed work has been translated into English, French, German, Polish, Italian and other languages. Mehrangiz's first pamphlet in English, *The Planet of Immortals*, was published by Exiled Writers Ink in 2021. At an international poetry festival in France, she was given the title 'The Dawn of Literature' in the culture section of *Le Temps*.

Some of Mehrangiz's poems in this book are translated from Farsi by the poet herself and edited by Catherine Davidson. Some are translated by Robert Chandler.

Stoning

Throw stones
Throw stones
At lewd
debauched
            criminal me!
                        Throw stones!

I was all in red
            Stone me
My clothes were the colour of my blood
                                    Stone me
Blood- red is rude
                  Stone me
My long hair longed for air
                  Stone me
But we can't have air here
                      Stone me
My footsteps called out
                      Stone me
Sound excites lust
                  Stone me
My eyes
  fell upon
            a man
                  Stone me
Seeing is forbidden

Stone me

Kissing is forbidden

Stone me

Drinking is forbidden

Stone me

Sobriety is forbidden

Stone me

The past is forbidden

Stone me

The future is forbidden

Stone me

I'm a woman

Stone me

I have eyes

Stone me

I have a tongue

Stone me

I have a brain

Stone me

You! who were not born of a mother!

I am a woman

Stone me

Stone me

stone...

stone...

stone...

Translated from Farsi by Robert Chandler.

Lash

Confess...   lash!
Confess...   lash!

Where is the stolen morning?
In the continent of blood!
Trying to be provocative?... lash!

In what state were you arrested?
I was stamping morning's passport
Smuggling contraband?... lash!

Where is your husband!
He's lost in his dark wedding-suit.
Wanting to ban marriage?... lash!

Where did you steal your fever?
Eh... Eh... From the wounds of day.
Coughing an ancient cough!... lash!

Display your dreams!
They've escaped.
Seize them!
They've sought asylum
Where?
In the navel of a star.
Which star?

The star of a fortunate tomorrow.
Trying to instil hope?… lash!

Your dreams have been seen.
Your thought clamour has been heard.
What do you have to say?
My fever… must have betrayed me.
Still don't surrender?… lash!

Say out loud what you're murmuring!
I can see you clearly in the darkness.
We'll take out your eyes… lash!
I can see with my skin.
We'll peel off your skin… lash!
I'll see with my bones.
We'll burn your bones… lash!
I'll see with my ashes.
We'll cast your ashes to the winds… lash!

You will multiply my eyes.
The sky will be full of my eyes
What will you do with the new buds?
With the birds?
With the water?
With yourself?
Put the air in quarantine?
Trying to be clever?…'Lash!

Where have you hidden your destiny?

In what follows on from day.
Needling night?… Lash!

Where have you stored the power of your hate?
Yesterday I sent it off to my child.
Your child? Ha-ha. Ha-ha.
We snuffed out his life… the day before yesterday!

…?! …?! …?!
May light…
May light… shine…
May light shine… on his place.

What was your father's job?… lash!
He ran the length of his ill-fortune.

Where is your mother?… lash!
The moment I was arrested, she left.
Where to?… lash!
To visit the grave of her hopes.
Where are her hopes?… lash!
Under your lash!
Laughing at us?… lash… lash… lash…
                                        lash…
                                                  la…sh
                                                            la…

…
Ha-ha Ha-ha Ha-ha
Her spirit laughed

Opened the stolen morning
Put her head on the horizon
And rolled
          onto the surface
                    of light!

Translated from Farsi by Robert Chandler.

Prisoner

Come and visit me
But
You won't get through the door
Doors have claws
Nor through the window
Panes can hurt

And the wall won't let you pass
No
Go to my shadow's house
Your knock
Will light up my shadow!

Translated from Farsi by Robert Chandler.

The Ten-Year-Old Bride

Forced into her starry dress as if
They had shaken the night
over her
And her murky tears
Suppurating from fear's sores

In a tribe with its mummified laughter
And quadruped hoof prints
On their sludge of imagination

The ten-year-old bride
Ten-year-old child
They drag… drag… drag her
to her husband's stronghold

Do you want your doll?
Your doll died!
Last night
Fairy tale giants
Mounted an assault
Murdered your father
Abducted your mother
Devoured your playmates
And your doll?
Crushed underfoot
… died!

But isn't she the ludicrous lineage of her mother?
A long wearisome chapter
An agonising likeness
taking refuge in her inner turmoil?

The bludgeon of inherited mores
on her head
The bludgeon of inherited fear and superstition
on her head
The bludgeon of inherited silence
on her head
Her today is buried
Under yesterday's debris
And maturity?
Like the convulsion of ancient marshes!

Where should she sleep?
To set her fearless dream… free

She felt
Her breath withering the flowers
I'm asleep
it's a nightmare!
I'm asleep
it's a nightmare!
tomorrow…
Tomorrow?!
Tomorrow's dawn
pitch black

The city turned upside down
Your father is an ogre
Your mother is a vampire
Your husband?
                    He is the demon of fairy tales!

…

And the dust
engulfed her so that
no one could see
the wind blowing her
                        … away

I Pass through the Mirror

I'm astonished at this garden
Kissing
the hand of autumn!

I'm astonished at this perfume
Sparkling itself
onto corpses

I'm astonished at this river
Flowing
into a marsh

I don't multiply in mirrors
I pass
through them!
I don't worry about what will happen to me

A tree
growing in a room
Doesn't think about the ceiling!

Another Type of Suicide

What a withered and hollow sky!
Human, is earth's masterpiece?
Ha-ha!
What creased, wrinkled words!
My mother's womb
Was more flourishing than this world
...
I folded life
And put it in my bag
saying: sorry God!
I acted like someone alive and hopeful
Shook hands with awaiting incidents
And through circumspect walls,
I passed
Like a lion
Surprised by an armed baby
I made the world surrender!
Hands up!
Empty Your Pockets!
Hollow medals of heroism
Fame without ownership
Fetid mornings of whorehouses
Ridiculous faces of religion
under the soot of lies
Queues of terrified prophets
apologising to people

Academic lusts of sterile scientists
Forced freedom of waves
Faithful torturers
Shredded protests
Mouldy jobs
Shining historical defeats
Unfinished chattering
Travelogues of internet tourists
Squeal of ideological mobiles
Squawking of postmodern poets
Scattered cigarette butts,
surrounding the thoughts of failed new-borns
Holy books, intercourse, toilet, condom
An empty bottle, famine, ax, bullet, vulture…
and blood
Blood spouting
from the pores of its pockets.
Puke!
The world fainted from the truth of my nausea
And I burst into laughter
at the impact of my nausea
Ridiculous unconsciousness!
Death to a world too weak
to overcome a smirk.
This is the retribution of the paltry rebellions of a coward!
Now here you are
corpse of the world!
It was obvious from when I was a sperm,
I would be suicidal!

Come through this Moment's Door

To the house of my poetry,
Come through this moment's door

Jealous ignorant spiders
Are Entangled
In the illusion of yesterday
And the delusion of tomorrow
In the weak construction of their webs!

The Planet of the Immortals

My spaceship speaks the truth
Earth is not a proper dwelling
Earth is a huge, decked-out zero

All that has passed
                    was playful misery
Like concurring while falling
Or laughing while vomiting
Or kissing while coughing

Our presence on earth
Was an irrelevant joke
Like the poet's irrelevance
                    to military ammunition
On earth
Only diseases… have a purpose
And only the dead
                    are all homeowners
And only the skeletons
                    are all smiling
Earth
The earth that like cancer
                    pretends to be stupid!

All of us
Offspring of hereditary intercourse

Constantly…
conquering deception
We believed our screams
Could make us immune
to earthquakes and storms
And only our corpses
made us identical!
We were buried in accordance with a sick law

On earth
God was being tortured
under the cloak of religion
Look!
Without any wind
Trees tremble with such confidence
As if they are precisely scared
Yes
They are scared, precisely!

Now
I invite you on a journey
You've been waiting a lifetime
to dream about it!
This journey
Is an eternal exemption… from bewilderment

Dear Companions!
Please wear special glasses made of 'Another Understanding'
These glasses

simplify formulas
Using these glasses
Is like eating forbidden fruit
So, you hot tempered earthly angels
Be on your guard!

Attention! Attention!
What was called 'love' on earth
At the end of this journey, is our host

Attention! Attention!
What was called 'body' on earth
Is not with us on this journey
The body was a seed
Sown on the earth
to scatter us
The body was a sign of the existence of distance!

Now you can see through your glasses
A fascinating war
between your memories
has broken out
and they have all surrendered!

That star luxuriating in glitter
Is a planet where
our arrival is being celebrated
And that vanishing spot
Is the earth

surrendering to an engulfing law

Now a pleasurable fear
captures our feelings
And we are going to be dissolved
In the radiance of perception
And a new human being
a new symbol
Steps on the 'Planet of the Immortals'
...
A woman brought you to the Earth!
And a woman took you from the Earth!

Woman's Miracle

Desert…
        and the incendiary sun…
But, woman's tongue is moist!

She licks the thorn's dream
Blossoms sprout on the tip of its claws

She licks the soil's dream
                    a fountain emerges
She licks the stone's dream
                    it bears fruit
She licks the dream of the driest leaf
                              taken by the wind
It jumps back on the bough

And woman?
Dances in heaven!

How Good to Be a Woman

I swear by the mighty morning
I swear by discerning hearts
I swear by the final human glance
That these words are the truth
And the truth
                    is in these words

When the stars become eyes
And the earth turns wholly into skin
And the moon screams
And the sun bathes its body
                                        triumphantly
How good…

When the bed
                    becomes men's pride
The bedsheet ripples stormy white
And everything speaks of a pure white clarity
The canary… sings white
The leaf falls white
The wind blows white
The snake turns its sting white
And the woman's skin glows
                                        from inner heat
How good…

When the ceiling stares at the bed
thoughtfully:
There is no honour
in being a ceiling
doomed to dry
When pleasure
spreads in its sacred breadth
And stars all turn green
And the sky
dresses in navy silk,
yearning for the red moon
And autumn, blue, moves out of orbit
How good…

The triangles of pleasure
Are measured by a tall subject
Acute angles
Form geometrical lines
venerated
And shadow breaks open, from illumination!
How good…

A lucky star is a lie
A lucky star is a cursed joy
Let's call lucky violet
Which is gold
and purple too!

How good to be a woman

When the woman
speaks golden and purple too!

How good to be a woman
When the woman
conquers the pen
And time pulls itself back
on both sides,
to open the way for love
And the angel of inspiration
begs the horizon:
Let me go and come back anew
And love opens the quotation mark:
The capacity of a dot
cannot be more than a dot
Little ones!
Zero does not rise
Little ones!
You hasty poets!
You poets pouring tears in a rush
Take pictures with your fame
as keepsake
Your fame is sterile.
And Bang! closes the quotation mark!

The woman takes prophets to bed… openly!

How good to be a woman
when the east, sun in its arms

look at the west wisely
And the woman
With divine bravery
rises
separates… from the earth
And caresses her radiant skin
And under the sternum of her power
She feels
palpitations of rich fertilization
And pleasure's froth
Spills out of her skin's pores
and she sings:
The crossing point, is woman
The power switch, is woman
The door latch, is woman
Wave, is woman
Mother earth, is woman
See how she gives birth… birth… birth…
Inhales love
And creates the best line of her Ghazal:
Human
Human: the king of the sonnet of the soil!
…
Don't let happiness drop from that bough!
Holy temptations!
Have you glued stars on your heads?

Hey Sun!
Darkness has covered its name with spangles

Grass! Grass!
What silky coquetry for the breeze!

Dance circulates in your waist
Dance then! Butterfly!

How good
How good
How good… to be a woman!

"In this collection Afghan and Irani women are centred. Their essential truths, their voices have been sought and collated. The Woman, Life, Freedom movement has been the most incredible women-led show of resistance in our lifetimes, and long may we remember. We cannot forget. Here in this anthology, we have some of the songs of freedom of brave, resisting souls. Through their work, we become better allies. Their pain becomes ours. Their suffering is our suffering. We cannot forget. No, we must not forget: Liberty does not come free to all. For many, many Afghani and Irani women, it has cost them their lives and continues to. Let us then celebrate in this moment, at this time the ten voices we have in our hands who have lived to tell the tale."
–**Sascha Aurora Akhtar**, thinker, writer and educator, author of *The Whimsy of Dank Ju-Ju*

Shirin Razavian

Shirin Razavian is a Tehran-born British poet whose work has appeared in *Poetry London, Index on Censorship, The London Magazine, Agenda* and *Persian Book Review,* among others. She has published six Farsi and English poetry collections in the UK, the latest of which is *Birds of Darkness.* Shirin is a member of the poetry magazine *World Cultural Heritage Voices,* and on the editorial committee of *Exiled Ink Magazine.* She was also a judge for the Jaleh Esfahani Cultural Foundation Poetry Prize. Some of her poems have been translated into Czech, in the anthology *Before Infinity Ends.* In 2015, Shirin was selected to represent Iran in the *Happiness-the Delight Tree,* an anthology published by the UN Society of Writers. Her work has also been featured in several other anthologies, including *The Poetry of Iranian Women* (US); *The Silver Throat of the Moon* (UK); *Resistance, Voices of Exiled Writers; Avay e Tabeed;* and *Diasporic Poetry.* Shirin has been a committee member of Iranian PEN in Exile, and Iranian Writers Association in Exile for four years. In 2023, she was chosen by Art on The Underground to collaborate with London artist Barby Asante in a project called *Declaration of Independence,* and received two Make a Difference awards for promoting diversity and inclusion.

Symphony of Fear

I am swallowed by the storm
When the thick, black liquid of dreams
engulfs my body that hangs off the bed
lifeless as a rag doll

I spin around
Carried further by the wind
Flying over the dry trees
With their brittle fingers
outstretched in palpable panic
A fine dust covers my dream
A herd of buffalo stampede over my head onto the barren planes
and the earth beneath me trembles under their hooves
Cold and damp hands grab mine
and take me further away

I see by the walls of the ruins
Women with charred faces squatting
their dead eyes staring into mine
I see children, their kidneys torn away for money

Men who have abandoned their soul
to sell their daughters to strangers, cheaply

I see houses, where love is traded at best price
and on their threshold, a sign reads 'Chastity'

I am carried further, spinning with the tornado
Young men are hanging from cranes
Performing a hideous pantomime with their bodies swinging back and forth

Crickets sing breathlessly in my ear
What will happen now, what will happen?
What will happen now, what will happen?
The wind ravishes and I sob uncontrollably

I wake up to a rainy morning
and a crow cawing bitterly outside my window

For Mahsa Amini

Your long hair
is the green song of freedom
and the words of the poem
that becomes a cry in the throat
Your bleeding body
will become the old pomegranate tree
that will tell the story of the rampage of the dry season
to every thirsty traveller
You have taken roots in that plagued land
The innocence in your eyes may become the gift of freedom for thousands
When the arabesque headscarves are swallowed by fire
and long strands of hair
Black, red and golden all meet the scissors
Long live life
Long live woman
Long live freedom
Long live us!

Published in: *HAIRAN: Poems of Hair and Freedom by Iranian Women in Times of Repression and Strugle* (Scotland Street Press, 2024)

Kiss

I kissed your soil
the day I left you,
the day I migrated away
with a suitcase
of spoken and unspoken pains.

I kissed your face
and a wish blossomed on my lips
till prayer became blessing

and the blue of the garden pool
and the silver tears
on the green leaves of the laudanum
became a part of my being.

And one chapter of me
remained behind
in your green alleyways.

There were many new days
and New Year's Days
came and went,
and you still continue
your parallel life in me.

Today
once again,
O living presence,
you sit with Hafez* and me
and a mirror and wine
and an apple, a coin, a hyacinth
and wheat grass, garlic, sumac and vinegar –
sib, seke, sonbol,
sabze, sir, somaq, serke –
our seven S-words that see in the Spring.

Translated from Farsi by Robert Chandler and the poet.

* Hafez was a 14th century Persian poet, highly celebrated for his lyric poetry (ghazal).

Don't You See?

Don't you see me
wandering the moors
with a dress made of the wind,
seaweed for my hair
and shoes made of the desert thorns?
Always mourning the transience of fleeting delights?
Don't you?
As the sun gives birth in my hands,
I gift it to the night
and donate the blooms of my life to death.
What do you see in the swaying of my pupils
if not my search for growth and enlightenment?
No one became the pathfinder on the plain of my wonder
Illumination only grew from the beads of sweat on my brow
I have never been the ivy, I won't
twist around you, but
I feel my slow descent in you
like
a
stone
in
water...

Waiting for Life

Waiting by the Rails
The coffee cup in front of me yawns
and the morning
sluggishly hangs last night's washed laundry
on the line of the horizon.
I sit patiently waiting for life and say:
Any day now, will pass by here
the old steam train called life
and I will get on and live
Patiently, I stare at the long rail of a thought
Lest the train of life passes me by.

Romina

In memory of Romina Ashrafi, a 13-year-old girl who became the victim of honour killing in Iran.

Romina is lying in a pool of crimson
A sickle has pierced her heart
Withered white wings of an angel, smeared
with blood, as though she has been
visited by the angel of death
The sickle glimmers in the moonlight
as Thirteen years of innocent life
drain away, one by one
Thirteen doves fly away with blood stained wing…
Romina was a good student
Romina was a kind daughter
The sickle belongs to her father
The blood had to be shed to restore honour
To wipe away the shame she has bestowed upon the family
Romina's body is now purified
To be honourably prayed for and buried
Romina's tears still glistening on her pale cheeks
Romina's honour is restored.

New Year

My new year starts
With howling wind
And whiplash of rain
The pale metallic face of the morning
Sickened by the faint yellow of a washed-out street light.

Life is back to normal, I say
getting ready to go to work.
I never mind the mundane
or the ordinary
I love the word 'Normal'.
All my life, I fought to fit into that window
to join the flocks of happy souls
living normal lives
with two happy parents
in a happy house with a happy cat.
Growing up without stabbings of depression or
displacement and oppression
not minding the politics or even the society
just living carefree as a red breasted robin on a holly branch.
All my life is haunted by the ghost of dreams and desires
of any normal girl
I have no regrets
some of those dreams turned to reality
late but not never.
Back at the office

In a grey St. James's Park
My window is speckled with rain drops
I work against the white noise
of colleagues speaking in calm voices
and the slushy sound of cars driving on wet asphalt.
Life is as grey and cool as the London sky
comforting with the aroma of coffee
and the green plant on my desk
eternally grateful for serenity.

Scent of a Poem

Sleeping last night
In dark-lightness
A poem seeping from my eyes onto my pillow
No strength to wake up
No strength to capture the fleeting words.
Every word
Scuttled away and hid in the tangles of my hair.
At dawn
When my mother greeted the sun
My pillow was poem-scented.
I said
The words have nested in the feathers of my pillow.

The Secret

They asked me to speak about
how we took on the sea and how
we climbed the mountain
How we speared down the monsters of the night
and galloped triumphantly into the dawn

They wanted me to tell the ship-wrecked
The despondent, the despairing and the downcast
How there is hope of survival
How we lived to tell the tale

They were seeking the potion, the method, the phial
The tincture, the amulet, the talisman
I said it wasn't in my gift to say
but I could give them a hint
Then I pointed to my heart.

Bride

My loneliness.
Do you know?
It lies
too deep inside me
even for you,
even for your clear eyes
to peel it from my body.

Where it lies hidden,
not even your kind hands
can seize it.
Bright spring of my sadness
where I wash each night
while the night bird
sings her sad, colourful songs.
Yes,
I am the bride of an awesome God.
Summoned night after night,
in silk and sequins and amber,
to the hall of sacrifice,
I rise each morning,
a pure slip of a girl,
from a bed
brimming with sunlight.

Translated from Farsi by Robert Chandler and the poet.

Muzhgan Saghar Schaffa

Muzhgan Saghar Schaffa was born in 1977 in Kabul, Afghanistan. Her father was in the army, and her mother was from the first generation of women's rights activists. She finished high school in Kabul, then following the Taliban's first round of invasion of Afghanistan, she emigrated to Germany. After learning German, she studied pedagogy, and now works with children. Her first collection of poetry, *Colourless Apples,* was published in Kabul in 2014, followed by two other collections, *The Sun Rains* and *Unsettled Ocean,* published in Herat in 2020.

Muzhgan's poems in this book are part of her collection of poetry, translated from Farsi into English by Rouhi Shafii.

Nothing

Nothing compensates you in me.
Nothing.
Nothing connects me to life,
except you.
You are dissolved in the most soothing sedatives
in the world.
Your presence postpones death,
and reflects life in a smile.

Return life to its original place.
If you turn away from me,
words will return to their original place.
Poems will be destroyed,
and scatter on the stoney road,
and crash under your masculine steps.
Kindness will wither away.

Be aware!
All your kisses will return to my lips,
and will be locked in my mouth.
I clench my teeth,
and submit my brain to 'hypnosis',
so to fall into an eternal ecstasy,
in an awakening coma,
with all I don't have of you
I begin to enter death.

Call the society of donation body parts,
and tell them she will not donate any parts,
with any price.
My heart is no good even to me.
I envelop myself in both hands,
fill my lungs with the scent of your body,
which I carried with me.

My eyes,
I leave them in the green and red gardens,
where you once took me.
You were my suicidal antidote,
far from reach.

Peak of Madness

I summarise in you,
at the climax of madness.
Here, there is no trace of betrayal.
I submerge in you,
Like a philosopher in his thoughts.

As I begin in you,
the history books will only talk of the cafes
you sat with me,
and the streets you walked with me,
and the dreams you dreamt with me.

How many springs and summers passed without you,
in the presence of the vine trees and the olive trees,
and a faraway village in southern Italy?

Who will speak of a mosquito bite,
which sank into my breast and wounded my soul
in deep regret....?
Autumn knows,
no leaf would fall from the tree
except your memory,
like a photograph cluster
from inside a flower.

No betrayal is involved.

I am imprisoned in the far north,
among the howling of dogs.
I repeat loyalty,
like the courtship of your scarf
with your neck.

No betrayal is involved.
Life is the second name for love,
and a stream running through,
the valley of death.

Without

Without traces of your feet,
I have lost all the roads
In the geography of the world.
Do not know the names of
the capitals of the world.

In your absence,
they will groove the earth,
close down borders,
and deprive the skies of lovebirds.

Without you,
no one will reach the centre of love,
and the streets of Paris
will be the continuation of
pointless shoes.

Without you, streets will reach dead ends,
and the roads will drown to the neck
in mirages.

Without you,
even the trees along the roads
sink into the earth,
instead of going backwards.

It was the traces of your feet
that connected me
to the romantic cities of the world.
I went along with you
to Damascus,
entered the coffee shops of Beirut.
And the Arab literature settled in my blood.
It was in an Arab desert
that I made you a shirt of kisses.

What did they do to me,
the traces of your feet?
What will they do to me
the traces of your feet?

Don't Bother!

Nothing can be changed.
Do not bother in vain.
Never ask me to not love you.

Can the warmth be taken away from the sun,
the rain from the clouds,
the colour from the moon,
the beauty from the flowers,
the flight from the swallows,
the silence from the night,
or
life from a crowded street?

Take the bread and water away from me,
not the desire to want you.
Take my sleep and wakefulness.
Not the beautiful feeling of loving you.
Like the undiscovered notes of a melody,
let you be played in me.
Let the love songs spread,
through the stony words of these dying times.

Glide with Me

Let me glide with you,
to the farthest point on earth,
to the other side of the waters,
in a street which hasn't reached the moon.

Let me hold you,
smell your body,
which has the fragrance of love,
and your masculine shoulders
which are my supporting beam.

I Did Not

I did not create poetry.
Poetry created me.
As a child, I did not play
in the rustling of the Autumn leaves.
On the onset of the cold winters,
dancing in the snowfall was forbidden!

How was pain born of me?
You, the dead womanhood of my childhoods!
My mother scared me of womanhood,
of poetry,
unaware that she gave birth to poetry.

Later, in an absurd contract,
they gave away my innocent, wheat-colour skin,
to a man, who has slept with hundreds of women.
They called poetry a whore.
I was poetry,
in the rhymes of a hundred women,
along with thousands of women,
who knew nothing of love,
nothing of womanhood.

On the streets, they saw me as a body.
Me, a body!
Wish a curtain could be drawn over their eyes.

Those ignorant of history.

In the crowded alleyways,
I was a moving poem,
in the guise of a whore,
not a woman in the sense of a love,
from becoming a woman in poetry,
to being torn apart,
in the disgraceful, swarm of their thoughts,
with lurid gazes.

In the river of life,
I stayed a woman,
when I breathed love.
I stayed a woman in love,
a woman being in love,
who, being called a whore,
that would not suit my tall figure.

Oh, what a strange time!
After the unsuccessful revolutions!
My father called my mother, *Hey, Mrs whore.*
My mother was an angel in the guise of a whore.
From my mother's whoredom,
to my innocence there were few steps,
along many bends and darkness,
and half a day,
from my mother's grave in Kabul,
to my mutilated body in Berlin,

in people's palates,
there was some whoredom distance,
some whoredom poetry,
some whoredom happiness.

Remember Me

Remember me,
at the end of the weeknights,
in the swarm of the parties.
Remember me,
as I scatter in the air
through the music notes.
Read me in a poem which reminds you,
of my orange skirt.
Breathe me in the smoke of your cigarette.
Take me inside your lungs.
Imprison me.
Put your hand round my neck.
In the invisible statutes of a burning woman.
Put your hand round my waist,
and dance with me.
Remember the taste of the kisses,
forgotten through years.
Remember me at the end-of-week parties,
when the green tea of memories,
would soothe your tiredness.

Drink me through the home-made wine,
and read my name,
which over weeks,
has skipped your memory.
Remember me in the flurry

of an end-of-week-party,
as I scatter through the music notes.
Read me in a poem which brings you the memory of,
my orange skirt.

Remember me among the smoke of your cigarette.
Put your hand round the neck of
various statutes of a woman,
who among your cigarette smoke,
dances softly and gently along with the angels,
and remember the taste of the kisses,
which you forgot through time.

My Sovereign,

I have commended to embalm you,
with the soil from my body,
so, I embrace you,
with the particles of my body,
more feminine than ever.
Who can be your Cleopatra
except me?

You Didn't

You did not write me a poem!
Was my womanhood less than Balqis Al-Rawi*?
No, it was not!
I, a bomb made of love exploded at your door.
Why did you never compare my lips to a red rose?
And why did you not taste the tip of my cherry earnings,
in the warmth of my body?
And why did you not compare the colours,
from my lips on your shirt,
which I had forgotten,
to the butterflies sitting on your shoulders?

Have you ever thought what happened,
to my frightened, shivering squirrels,
in the forest of the ethereal longing,
far from your mythological hands?

You did not call my name.
My name which is the most poetic ballade
in the history of women's names.
My name which was engraved,
on the horizon with
a golden colour.
What did you do with the falcon of my gaze,
which was wounded before it got,
to the field of your gaze,

and fell into the lagoon
of indifference?

The Kabul of my gaze is dripping blood.
You were involved in all my body's infightings.
You put my heart to fight with my liver,
and bloodied the gates of my soul,
and swam into my veins like a kingfish.
My longings,
my heart will burn your hands,
piece by piece.

What did I lack to all women of the world,
which you threw away my kisses,
like a frightened and bewildered sparrow,
away from the window of your lips,
into the darkness?

Now, be brave,
and snatch my kisses,
from the mouths of female Australian dolphins.
It is not too late.
Do not let them fall from the tip of my eyes,
to the most gruesome valley of forgetfulness.
Do not let me burn in hatred,
away from your kisses and making love.

Were I not your Aleida[**]?
I was one of your most innocent, scandalous lovers.

You never wrote a poem,
for the flowers on my skirt.
Flowers which withered away
before the spring of your arrival.

After me,
the sun will not shine on you,
and darkness will fall on you,
and no woman will write a poem,
for the smoke from your cigarette,
and the buttons on your shirt,
and the scent of your body,
And your Che Guevara style shirt.

Tell me,
hero of my tales,
shall I love you still?
Cause…
I still love you.

* Balqis Al-Rawi was the wife and muse of Syrian poet Nizar Qabbani.

** Aleida March was Che Guevara's wife.

Naked Women

In me, there are women,
who have hidden their nakedness,
so not to cry out centuries' voices.
Naked women who wake up with me,
hide their nakedness from me.
Laugh,
cry,
and call on you.

"This is a very powerful anthology, the voices of the ten poets, so different from each other, explore the past and present, the seen and unseen, capturing the immense personal grief and collective struggle in Iran and Afghanistan over the last four decades. It is immensely hard to summarise what is contained in the anthology, the poems are powerful and unforgettable."

–**Janet Sutherland**, poet, author of *Home Farm*

"The poems in *Songs of Freedom* are a deep and moving poetic education for any reader. These works, by leading women poets from Iran and Afghanistan are parables of survival, frequently honouring those who were less fortunate, who did not survive, they poignantly bear witness. At times direct as transmission, but also linguistically playful, these powerful voices lift from the page, inhabiting the world at large as part of a continual struggle, a poetic resistance to centuries of male-dominated oppression."

–**James Byrne**, poet, editor and translator, author of *Places You Leave*

Rouhi Shafii

Rouhi Shafii is a sociologist, writer, translator of Persian poetry, and women's rights activist. She has published six books, both in Farsi and English. Among her acclaimed translations into Farsi are *Women of Vietnam* and *Argentina, National Resistance and Peron's Dictatorship*. Her memoir, *Scent of Saffron* (1997) was widely welcomed as one of the first memoirs in English by an Iranian woman after the revolution. Her historical novel, *Pomegranate Hearts* (2006) was a kaleidoscope of fiction within the history of contemporary Iran. She has published reviews on the memoirs of a number of political prisoners in both Farsi and English. She has translated two books of Persian poetry into English, *Migrating Birds* and *The Anthems of Love,* both published by the Jaleh Esfahani Cultural Foundation. Her latest book, *Gates to the Great Civilization* in Farsi was published in 2023. Rouhi is a member of the Executive Committee of Exiled Writers Ink, and the editorial board of *Exiled Ink Magazine.* Her first collection of poetry in English will soon be published.

The Beginning

I am sitting on the terrace of my apartment
in Spanish Andalusia, sipping tea.
The Sierras can be seen from a distance.
The peak sits motionless, spreading its wings over the horizon.
The sky is deep blue, soon turning grey
as the autumn nears.
Then, I will be long gone back to London.
Something flickers in my mind.
Are these Sierras home to my imagination?
Is this the reason I love this spot so much?
Maybe I am looking at the mountain peaks of Damavand?
There, when I left home, they were covered in snow.
Here, the rocky Sierras of Andalusia are dry and grey.
Still!

The Scriber

Everything comes to an end.
The breeze whispered to the weeping willow.
Our tale, was written on the bricks of a dead-end street
In a Spanish old town, where I was once walking
on a narrow road.
The houses looked like ancient colourful boxes.
Flowers hanged from every corner and crack.
A door was open as I passed by.
The walls were covered in orange and blue tiles.
An old woman was sitting motionless,
leaning to the wall.
She summoned me to sit by her side.
And told me the tale of an unfinished love,
written on the bricks of that dead-end street.
A scribbler has painted some colourful scribes:
Hey, you the wanderer,
Should you walk through this lane,
Hand in hand with your lover,
Slow your pace and take a deep breath,
And let the world pass by you in wonder.
You never know which one,
The one who knew love,
Or the one who never knew
Walked this road in happiness.
The old woman closed her eyes,
and let me read to the end.

You the reader of this scribe,
Walk on the road with a smile on your face.
You happened to face a question no one else did.

Outside

The wind is howling.
Winter rain splashing.
Darkness stepping into my room,
deep into the irises of my eyes,
and creeping into my heart.
Lights are hidden deep,
into the darkness.
Cold air seeps through the cracks of the window seal.

Darkness forms different shapes.
The words you spoke,
in the passing words,
and I drove by them,
on my high horse.

Inside the minds of those,
who stand in a circle,
in the shadow of an early morning,
in the year zero,
to watch a young man,
who was a child when the crime
was committed,
and now at eighteen, is hanged from a crane.
As his body dances to the symphony of death,
which is played on the loudspeakers,
and the shadows move behind the horizon,

the onlookers, satisfied, sit for breakfast,
before going about their business,
as usual.

These days my friend,
darkness chants into the microphones
of the mosques,
in my occupied homeland,
which in another life used to chant,
hymns of peace, love and life.

Finally!
Through the cracks of the frozen earth,
my heart,
my cold, dead heart,
feels shadows of doubt moving away,
as darkness shivers on the onset of light,
and I hold my face to the window,
which is splashing light into my room.

Perhaps

Perhaps I should go to the beginning and rename the road,
or erase the memory of destination altogether.
Perhaps I should sit at the edge of the river,
where the water gushes from the unknown,
and wash your face and your gaze
in the thunder of desire.
Perhaps I should write your name on a leaf,
and float it over the running water,
or, put it under the wings of a white pigeon,
to take it away from destination.
Perhaps you will remember that summer night,
on that faraway rooftop,
and a kiss which froze at the chill of dawn.
Perhaps you will knock at my door one day,
and the scent of memories, erased through time
find their way into the rose garden.
Perhaps I loved you once,
or you loved me once,
both burnt in the chaos of confusion.

How Many Years

In memory of Dr surgeon Parisa Bahmani, who was shot dead in a peaceful demonstration of doctors during the Woman, Life, Freedom movement.

How many years does it take for your hands
to learn how to cut in precision and remove
a malignant tumour from the body of a human?
How many years does it take for you,
the beautiful Parisa Bahmani, to sit in a classroom,
to stand round the dissection room,
to learn about every tissue and cell in a body,
so tomorrow you can save a life?
The life of a child, a young man, an old woman,
even the life of your enemy as you are committed
to saving lives.
You, the woman surgeon who stood in protest
for the lives lost for life, for liberty.
You, the woman, who stood up for us all.
You, whose hands saved lives,
whose life perished in the mayhem of blood for life.
Did you not once save the life of the soldier
who shot you out of rage or ignorance?
Or, maybe saved his mother, or sister,
as he brought them to your hospital and begged you
to give them back their shining eyes,
and you did, as you were taught to save lives.

Now, those skilful hands, that thoughtful brain,

that smile of satisfaction as a life came to life,
is lifeless in a morgue.
Now, we know, your loved ones know,
and the world knows that cruelty has no boundaries,
that rage cuts through humanity,
that pure ignorance, pure hatred,
aims its gun to kill, you the woman.
They took your life, and your liberty
as a woman.
You, Parisa, the woman, the doctor surgeon,
the life saver of that shooter who shot you,
your name will sit embroidered side by side
with all the women who lost their lives
for freedom,
for life.
You the Woman!

Grieving Mother

In memory of Mohsen Shekari who was executed for a crime he did not commit.

In this cold, dark night,
voices mingle with images,
with the speed of sound,
traveling from home,
reaching to cloud my memory.

The howling of a grieving mother.
Was it before or after?
Filled the streets
and spilled into town
and travelled through the waves
and wires
across the globe,
to reach the pale moon,
and then my bewildered soul.

Was it before or after she heard
her young boy has been slaughtered
that her heart ripped apart,
and her cries reached that pale moon?
The pale moon!
The pale moon!
Witness of our dark history!

I closed the window,

switched off the radio, threw the paper out,
not to know of her pain,
unbearable, piercing pain,
of losing her boy to nothingness.

Would he be the last?
I wonder!
Who was the first?

What was the name of number one thousand eight hundred
young man facing the firing squad?
I know the names of the last ones,
those teenage girls who were shot in the dark.
The ones whose mothers' screams,
made the stars hide from sight
and shame covered the milky way.

I keep it as a secret,
I wash it in the tears of all mothers,
who lost their soul in grief,
in pain and in waiting to see the day
all hanged men be hanged one by one,
or all in one.

The stains never wash.
The pain never lessens.
Those murdered never return.
Even if we send all the hanged men to be hanged.
And that my friend is the saddest
part of our tragedy.

War Zone

A narrow bridge connects two hearts together.
A bridge where the river flows underneath.
The moonlight dances with the waves as the night falls.
Two young lovers, one from each nation
used to cross the bridge,
once in the morning,
and once in the afternoon
after work.
They would reach in the middle
and become one whole body.
A wounded soldier is wandering
on the same half burnt bridge
looking for his missing arm.
A mother's gaze is frozen on the western side of the river,
as a bloated corpse
swam down the stream.
Could it be her golden-haired youngster,
whose laughter shook their shabby cottage
as he returned from school?
The thunder of war planes engulfs the silence.
Fire rains down overhead.
A drone hidden from sight
registers every moment for the military men
with bloated bellies
and greedy eyes to look at the photo
taken by the drone.

Of the two lovers, one went to fight in the war
with his lover, who turned enemy overnight.
The poet who wrote their tale
has broken her pen and spilled the ink
over the wall to cover the
'Death to the enemy' graffiti.
She never wrote love songs again.
The gypsies never danced on the bridge
which connected the two cities.
Years later, when the conflict ended
and both sides united to condemn the fire bearers,
I sat on a hillside,
where I could see the view from both
north and south.
The silence broke by the thunder of music
from a carnival and I thought
how can we ravage our humanity over nothingness?

Published in: *Ukraine in the Work of International Poets* (Literary Waves Publishing, London / PoEzja Londyn, 2022)

The Encounter

I was walking on that crowded street
looking for a memory of the past,
unaware that far beyond the horizon
time has erased my world.

Then the echo of your steps
one by one,
resounding in my heart,
the music of Gods.
One step forward and two steps into the mist.

I heard someone call my name
It wasn't you
Someone stole your smile
It wasn't me
Your smile wasn't there on your lips
Nothing reached me
You and your smile
reached your destination.
I never did.

From among the crowd
your voice echoed in the mist
I know, I know you were there,
here, right at that moment in time.

But as the mist cleared,
the faces appeared
one by one.
I was there,
but you and your smile
were there no more.

The Walls

Two on either side
behind the concrete,
they collide over me.

The first on my left hides the home I left,
in haste, in despair
and hope,
as my mother's tears
washed my traces away.

Behind the one on my right
dreams are dormant.

Walking the length of the desert
in hasty strides,
out of fear, hunger and hopelessness,
and in slow motion,
hope.

The sun burns the skin,
the palm trees wither away,
the oasis dries up,
and the sand storm envelopes me.

Hope walks away backwards.
Two steps forward might take me to destination.

One step lingers in doubt.

The wall on my right, where my dreams
have travelled faster than me
can be seen in the haze.
I see no door, no key and no light
to show the way forward.

Walking to the north,
back to the south,
back to the first stop
silence envelopes the desert behind.

I am in no man's land,
stranded between two walls.

This poem was inspired by Goran Baba Ali's novel, *The Glass Wall* (Afsana Press, London, 2021)

For You, Blue

To honour the memory of my late friend, Mehri Jafari, who slid down a glassier in a climbing expedition in Kyrgyzstan in 2021, I include this poem, *For You, Blue* which was written by her in Farsi and translated by me into English.

Bring your face forward.
Your eyes, colour of the Channel sea.
Blue, blue, khaki green, darker than the southern storms.
The winds that come from faraway oceans.
Bring your face forward.
when I look,
hundreds of tiny fish,
hundreds of tiny fish.

Between us a broken Cross and a broken Allah!
Hands handcuffed in the back,
and a black blindfold.
Do you know her?

My hands reach the other side of the Thames,
and water flows, flows.
Is this the blue sky, or the blueness of water from your eyes?
I squeeze it,
and your mouth smells of the sharks in the North.
Wetter than a coastal home in the Caspian.
Sweeter than the Sabalan honey.
My blue,
rising from the lake.

Let me swim in your arms.
Let me get old in your corner.
My river, my beating heart.
My beating heart.
Flow, do not rot still.
Do not get salty.
Flow, flow, flow.

I let you pass through me.
Floods of water,
say something about you.
Something that reminds me of you.
Years, years later.
Now with those poems and erased in your arms.
Not with the twitching of my eyelids,
when I think of you.

I want to row in your gaze,
to turn round and round,
in your blue, blue gaze,
till I forget the Salt Lake.

"This ground-breaking anthology is a document of humanity finding its voice in the harshest circumstance – when not only humanity, but also its gender is persecuted, abused, tortured, and crushed. In the same time, it proves once again how right was Paul Celan to assert that poetry is the proof that human beings can be tortured and even killed – but they can never be destroyed. Language remains and it bears witness. Like other seminal anthologies documenting historic and individual traumas (I am thinking first of all to the one edited by Carolyn Forché in 1993, *Against Forgetting: 20th Century Poetry of Witness*, or to *Language for a New Century: Contemporary Poetry from the Middle East, Asia, and Beyond*, edited by Tina Chang, Nathalie Handal, and Ravi Shankar in 2008), this anthology collecting the voices of ten Iranian and Afghan women poets is another memorable proof of this axiom: barbarity will never have the final word. Our entire humanity rests on such proofs. And on such anthologies."

–**Radu Vancu**, poet and novelist, President of PEN Romania, author of *Transparența*

"This wonderful anthology of deeply moving poems by brave women, forged in the white heat of oppression and exile, speaks to the power of poetry to inspire and transform pain into liberation. *Songs of Freedom* embodies the suffering and dreams of the women of Iran, Afghanistan and the world in precise words and scorching harmonies that rise up against power-hungry politicians and clerics who are offended by the laughter of children and the glow of the full moon at midnight, who would cover up their crimes against the freedom of women, attack the spirit of life and suppress love and sensuality under the disguise of religion. These inspiring and painful poems transform cruelty and suffering into revelatory visions that lift our spirits and open doors to love, understanding and liberation. This anthology is a celebration of life, love, and truth by pointing to the path of liberation through universal beauty."

–**John Curl**, writer and poet, author of *Revolutionary Alchemy*

"The subjugated condition of women in Iran and Afghanistan is well known. In order to speak or write, many women have moved abroad. But emigration in such circumstances is not easy. This anthology of ten prominent women writers living in exile carries their experience, some through translation, into ours. There are marvellous poets here. The book is full of absence and desire. It will haunt you."
–**George Szirtes**, poet and translator, author of *The Photographer at Sixteen*

"These poems by Afghan and Iranian women writers in exile are a poignant and moving record of recent persecution and subjection. What is most striking about the anthology as a whole is that these women seem to share a language of resistance that braids lyric voice and reverie to the hard facts of lived experience. Remarkably, however, the lyricism never softens the impact of the physical and mental violence at their core but rather accords it a resonance, a dreamlike quality that carries it deep into the hearts of listeners and readers alike. Through the powerful deployment of clearly original voices – some of which are ably conveyed by the translators into English – this anthology will give anyone contemplating the embattled situations of women in Afghanistan and Iran a sense of hope. These are voices that sing while they reprimand, lament and upbraid."
–**David Kinloch**, poet, author of *In Search of Dustie-Fute*